6.95

KATE DiCAMILLO

KATE DiCAMILL

Flora & Ulysse
The Illumin
Adven

KATE
DiCAMILLO

ILLUSTRATED BY K.G. CAMPBELL

CHILDREN'S
STORYTELLERS

Kate DiCamillo

by Christina Leaf

BLASTOFF!
4
READERS

BELLWETHER MEDIA · MINNEAPOLIS, MN

Note to Librarians, Teachers, and Parents:

Blastoff! Readers are carefully developed by literacy experts and combine standards-based content with developmentally appropriate text.

Level 1 provides the most support through repetition of high-frequency words, light text, predictable sentence patterns, and strong visual support.

Level 2 offers early readers a bit more challenge through varied simple sentences, increased text load, and less repetition of high-frequency words.

Level 3 advances early-fluent readers toward fluency through increased text and concept load, less reliance on visuals, longer sentences, and more literary language.

Level 4 builds reading stamina by providing more text per page, increased use of punctuation, greater variation in sentence patterns, and increasingly challenging vocabulary.

Level 5 encourages children to move from "learning to read" to "reading to learn" by providing even more text, varied writing styles, and less familiar topics.

Whichever book is right for your reader, Blastoff! Readers are the perfect books to build confidence and encourage a love of reading that will last a lifetime!

This edition first published in 2016 by Bellwether Media, Inc.

No part of this publication may be reproduced in whole or in part without written permission of the publisher. For information regarding permission, write to Bellwether Media, Inc., Attention: Permissions Department, 5357 Penn Avenue South, Minneapolis, MN 55419.

Library of Congress Cataloging-in-Publication Data

Leaf, Christina.
  Kate DiCamillo / by Christina Leaf.
    pages cm. – (Blastoff! Readers: Children's Storytellers)
  Summary: "Simple text and full-color photographs introduce readers to Kate DiCamillo. Developed by literacy experts for students in second through fifth grade"– Provided by publisher.
  Includes bibliographical references and index.
  ISBN 978-1-62617-339-2 (hardcover : alk. paper)
  1. DiCamillo, Kate–Juvenile literature. 2. Authors, American–21st century–Biography–Juvenile literature. 3. Children's stories–Authorship–Juvenile literature. I. Title.
PS3604.I23Z75 2016
813'.6–dc23
  [B]
                          2015030694

Table of
Contents

Kate DiCamillo is an author who has touched the hearts of many readers. Her stories of hope and love have become children's book **classics**. They have also won her two **Newbery Medals**.

"**There is no right or wrong way to tell a story.**"
Kate DiCamillo

Even with all her success, Kate stays **humble**. She loves telling stories and sharing her work with kids around the world!

Katrina DiCamillo, or Kate, was born on March 25, 1964, in Philadelphia, Pennsylvania. She often fell sick as a child.

"When we read together, we connect. Together, we see the world. Together, we see one another."
Kate DiCamillo

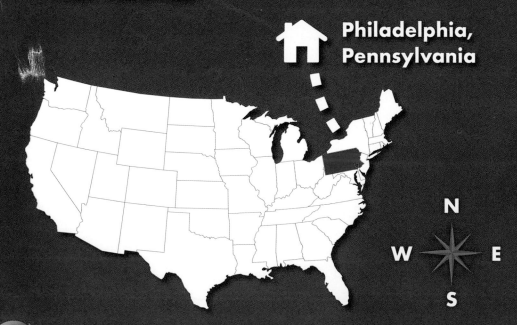

Philadelphia, Pennsylvania

At age 5, she moved to Florida with her
mother and older brother. Her family
hoped the warm weather would help
Kate's health.

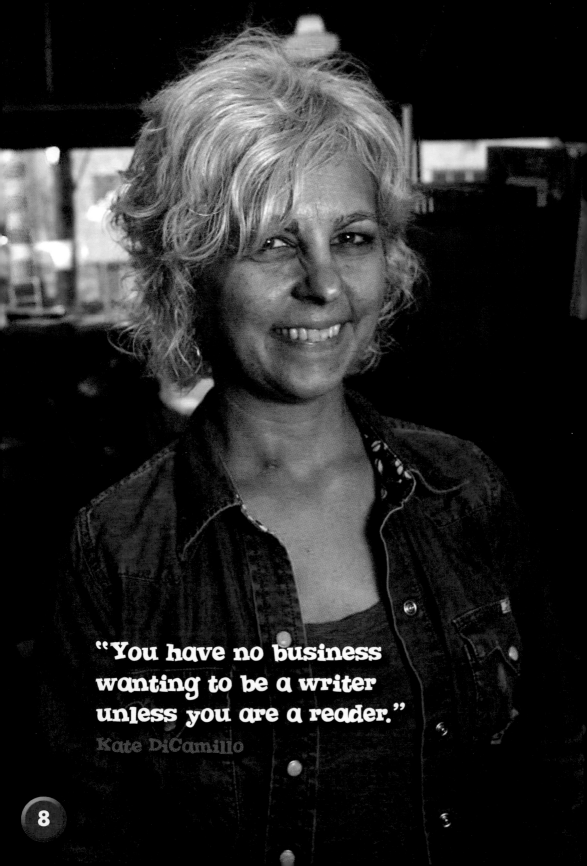

"You have no business
wanting to be a writer
unless you are a reader."
Kate DiCamillo

Still, Kate struggled with illness in Florida. She stayed home from school a lot. To keep busy, she read anything she could. The librarian in her hometown named her a "True Reader."

Kate went on to study English in college. There, a professor told her she was a good writer.

ANNA SEWELL
A spirit that would not be broken...
BLACK BEAUTY
The Autobiography of a Horse
COMPLETE AND UNABRIDGED

fun fact

The story of *Black Beauty* made Kate very sad when she was young. She swore to never read another book with an animal on the cover. Now most of her books are about animals!

Kate liked the idea of being a writer. She decided it would be her **career**. She worked odd jobs for about ten years and planned to write outside of work. However, she actually wrote very little during that time.

By 1994, Kate knew she needed a change. She moved with a friend to Minneapolis, Minnesota. There, she began writing every day.

fun fact

One of Kate's jobs after college was at Walt Disney World. She told people to watch their step as they got off a ride.

10

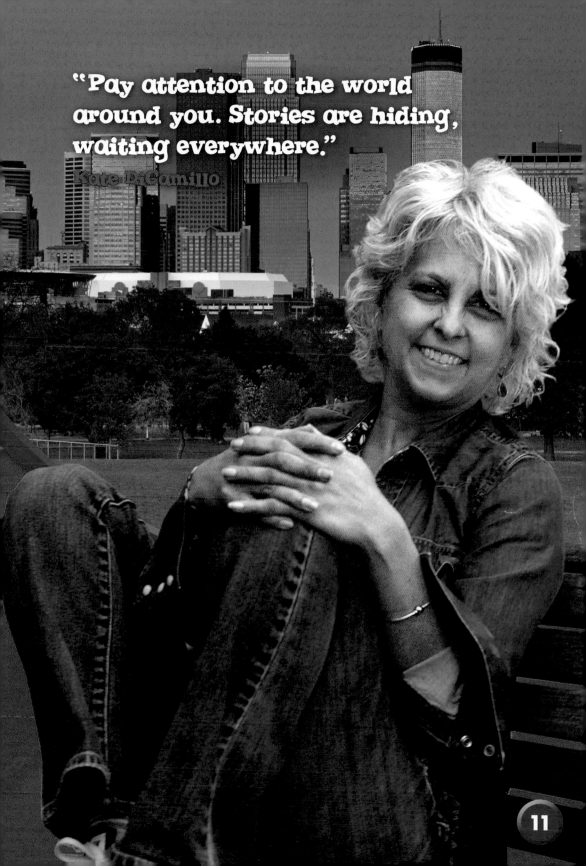

"Pay attention to the world around you. Stories are hiding, waiting everywhere."

Kate DiCamillo

In Minneapolis, Kate got a job at a book **distributor**. She worked in the children's section and read the books when she could.

Minnesota was a lot different than Florida. One cold, awful winter, Kate felt homesick. She began writing a story filled with things that she missed. It was set in Florida and featured a big, lovable dog.

fun fact

Kate read *The Watsons Go to Birmingham–1963* at her job in Minneapolis. She loved it and copied the first chapter at home. She was trying to find out what made it so good.

CHRISTOPHER PAUL CURTIS
WINNER OF THE NEWBERY MEDAL & THE CORETTA SCOTT KING AWARD

THE WATSONS GO TO BIRMINGHAM
–1963

Kate wrote a picture book that she hoped would be **published**. By chance, Kate had an editor at Candlewick Press look at her work. But the book was eventually **rejected**.

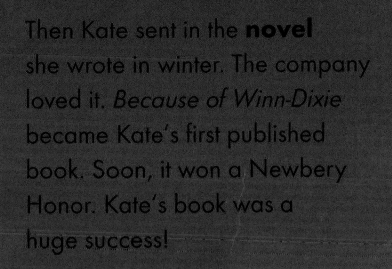

Then Kate sent in the **novel** she wrote in winter. The company loved it. *Because of Winn-Dixie* became Kate's first published book. Soon, it won a Newbery Honor. Kate's book was a huge success!

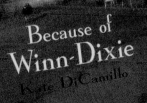

fun fact

Kate sticks to a writing schedule. She wakes up early and writes two pages a day, five days a week.

Kate has since written picture books, chapter books, and novels. Each book is different. However, many have similar **themes**.

SELECTED WORKS

Because of Winn-Dixie (2000)

The Tiger Rising (2001)

The Tale of Despereaux (2003)

Mercy Watson to the Rescue (2005)

The Miraculous Journey of Edward Tulane (2006)

The Magician's Elephant (2009)

Bink & Gollie (2010) (with Alison McGhee)

Flora & Ulysses: The Illuminated Adventures (2013)

Leroy Ninker Saddles Up (2014)

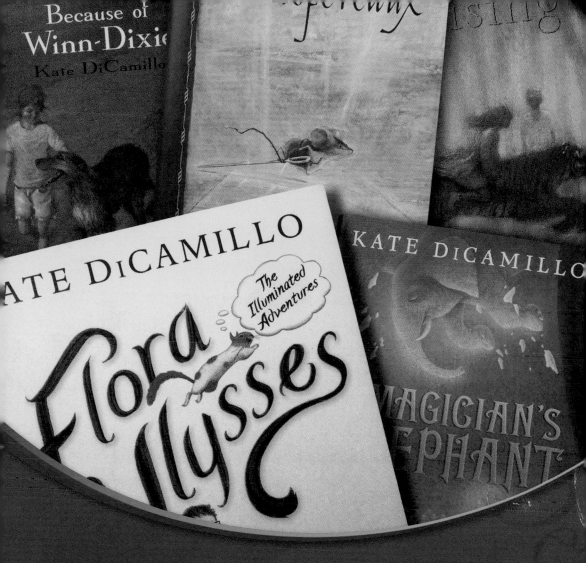

Kate's books are often **whimsical**. Her writing is **realistic** yet playful. Colorful characters fill her stories, including a silly dog, a brave mouse, and a heroic squirrel. The occasional hint of magic brightens everyday situations.

Sometimes, Kate's books are sad. Her characters often deal with loss or loneliness. Many readers can **relate** to these feelings. It helps to know that there are others who feel the same way.

Her books are also filled with hope. Characters make unlikely friends. They find the good in tough situations.

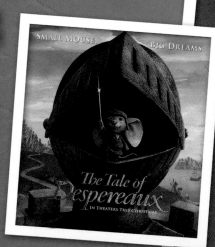

POP CULTURE CONNECTION

In 2008, *The Tale of Despereaux* movie hit theaters. The film's beautiful images helped the Newbery Medal book come to life.

"Almost everybody's interesting if
you give them a chance and if you
ask them the right questions."
Kate DiCamillo

Kate's books have made a big impact on children. Some kids say *Winn-Dixie* or *Despereaux* is the reason they became readers. For Kate, this is as good as any award.

IMPORTANT DATES

1964: Kate DiCamillo is born on March 25.

2000: *Because of Winn-Dixie*, Kate's first novel, is published.

2001: *The Tiger Rising* is named a National Book Award Finalist.

2004: *The Tale of Despereaux* wins the Newbery Medal.

2005: The first Mercy Watson book comes out.

2007: *Great Joy*, Kate's first picture book, is published.

2008: *The Tale of Despereaux* movie plays in theaters.

2010: Kate publishes *Bink & Gollie* with her friend, Alison McGhee.

2014: *Flora & Ulysses: The Illuminated Adventures*, Kate's novel with comic book elements, wins the Newbery Medal.

2014: Kate is named the National Ambassador for Young People's Literature by the Library of Congress.

In 2014, Kate was named an **ambassador** for children's books. The job involves helping people remember the joy of reading. Her next novel should be a good reminder!

Glossary

ambassador—an official representative or messenger

career—a job someone does for a long time

classics—works that will remain popular for a long time because of their excellence

distributor—a company that supplies stores with books

humble—not too proud or thinking that you are better than other people

Newbery Medals—awards given each year to the best American children's books; the Newbery Medal is given to first place and the runners-up receive Newbery Honors.

novel—a longer written story, usually about made-up characters and events

published—printed for a public audience

realistic—like real life

rejected—turned down

relate—to connect with and understand

themes—important ideas or messages

whimsical—imaginative and playful, often with a sense of humor

To Learn More

AT THE LIBRARY

Corbett, Sue. *Kate DiCamillo*. New York, N.Y.: Marshall Cavendish Benchmark, 2013.

DiCamillo, Kate. *The Tale of Despereaux: Being the Story of a Mouse, A Princess, Some Soup, and a Spool of Thread.* Cambridge, Mass.: Candlewick Press, 2003.

Shea, Therese. *Kate DiCamillo: Newbery Medal-Winning Author.* New York, N.Y.: Britannica Educational Publishing, 2016.

ON THE WEB

Learning more about Kate DiCamillo is as easy as 1, 2, 3.

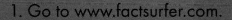

1. Go to www.factsurfer.com.

2. Enter "Kate DiCamillo" into the search box.

3. Click the "Surf" button and you will see a list of related web sites.

With factsurfer.com, finding more information is just a click away.

Index